THE INSURANCE UX SURVIVAL GUIDE

A FIELD GUIDE FOR BUILDING DIGITAL EXPERIENCES THAT EXCEED EXPECTATIONS

STEVE JOHNSON

Book Cover and all illustrations by Steve Johnson

First Edition, 2025

ISBN 9798218847074 (Paperback)

ISBN 9798218847098 (eBook)

This survival guide, intended for insurers, MGAs, Mutuals, agents, and anyone with a love of insurance, is based on over 20 years of insurance and UX experience, insights from over 250,000 customers, and everything that we've seen building insured.io from the ground up.

Contents

Preface

First off, thank you for picking up a copy of this book. It's been something of a labor of love, and a challenge to find the time to balance business, life, and writing, while also completely avoiding AI for content. I haven't written this much on a single subject since college, and it was a lot easier to write when there was a grade on the line! This is a book I have wanted to put together for a long time. I have lived and breathed insurance technology since I started my professional career over 20 years ago (after slinging pizzas for a few years), and while I, with an amazing team, have built a successful company around this very subject, I believe that some knowledge should be open source.

Just a little about my background, to add some context. After the aforementioned pizza years, I started my insurance career as a commercial lines policy processor, somewhere in the early 2000s, for a company called Allied Insurance. I spent my days hitting F keys in a green screen system, manually entering data, calculating rates, and filling out a lot of forms. They were acquired by Nationwide, and while there, I quickly moved on to underwriting. As I often joke, I wasn't very good at it, and so after I parted ways with Nationwide (or, more accurately, they parted ways with me) I accidentally found my way into insurance technology while working for a company called Stonewood Insurance, a non-standard auto Managing General Agency (MGA) in 2005. While there, I worked on everything from rating algorithms, to billing systems, to policy documents, to insured websites, as I moved from technical analyst to software developer. When that company was acquired, a small group left to set out on our own, founding TundraLogic, and making our way in Insurtech as developers for hire, building interfaces for agents, consumers, underwriters, and customer service, for nearly every line of P&C insurance. From this, partly because professional are exhausting, we launched the ins ured.io Customer Engagement Platform in 2019, pivoting from custom software to software-as-a-service. From underwriter to software developer to Chief Product Officer, I have been focused on designing, creating, and building successful insurance user experiences for practically my entire career.

I have seen my fair share of generational shifts in insurance technology. From paper apps, to green screens, to those horrible gradients that people loved so much in 2008. From Excel spreadsheets to AI, insurance has changed so much over the last two and a half decades. Every few years, there has been a new "digital transformation" push, and it's often the insured that feels the pain of every new and different idea. Changing core systems, implementing disparate technology over multiple years, and constantly changing expectations have fractured the customer experience for many carriers. That is one of the reasons that insured.io has been successful. We take the customer experience out of the hands of insurance company executives and overworked in-house developers, bridge disparate systems together, and bring our years of expertise to carriers and MGAs that struggle with continuously keeping up.

As I said, despite building a company around this, good UX shouldn't just be our secret sauce. I want this information to be readily available for the masses. I have put this book together in order to somewhat open-source my brain (I warned you), and share what we have learned over the years regarding the ever-changing UX landscape, with best practices, helpful tips, and some great data that we have collected over the years. This handbook is not necessarily an instruction manual, editorial, or (I promise) a sell-sheet. I have intended this to be a helpful (survival) guide for any insurer on their UX journey, with data, analysis, anecdotes, experience, and hopefully a little bit of entertainment, in order to share what the modern insurance customer really cares about. My hope is that you will take away from this at least a few ideas on how to kick-start your next generation of digital transformation.

Thanks for reading,

Steve Johnson
Founder & Chief Product Officer, insured.io
steve@insured.io
https://www.linkedin.com/in/steve-johnson--

Part I

UX: An Introduction

Definitions

User Experience (UX): *A person's overall interactions and feelings about a product, system, or service, encompassing its utility, ease of use, efficiency, and emotional impact. The overall journey.*

User Interface (UI): *The specific touchpoints where a user interacts with a product, something visual, tactile, and interactive. Buttons, menus, screens, icons, layout, and visual design.*

UX vs UI

UX and UI are terms that you will sometimes see used interchangeably, and while they are related to one another, they inform very different parts of the customer journey. UX, particularly when it comes to customer interactions with a business, is often relegated solely to the usability of a website, portal, or similar online experience. If only it were that simple. While those are indeed important, UX encompasses far more than just what we see on the screen.

UX scales out exponentially, and is vastly larger than just a single process, site, or workflow. UX is the **entire interaction** with your product, from beginning to end. It spans the purchasing process, customer service, documentation, onboarding, offboarding, communication, touch points, and the entirety of each and every sub-interaction as well. It is the entire lifecycle, and it doesn't matter if it's a physical product, a service, or an app. There is a psychology to UX because there is true emotional impact to a user's experience, which seems intense, but can be easily understood when you see how a user's emotional response is reflected in star ratings, reviews, likes, or even just "love it," "hate it," or "meh" about it. It seems obvious, but a customer's sum of interactions with a product or service informs their feelings about it directly, which is why it is so important to understand what is part of UX. In fact, your entire team is part of the User Experience, not just your designers and developers. Business strategy, marketing, customer service agents, and finance all play a role in the overall user experience, because each one of those may be a touch point between you and your customer. If a bill is difficult to understand, which in turn makes a customer unsure of what to pay, which leads them to call customer service and be placed on hold.... You get the idea. The usability and speed of your website are components of UX, though they begin to fall far more under the definition of UI.

If UX is driving, then UI is the steering wheel. It's part of UX, certainly, and a crucial part, but it isn't the whole thing. UI is the particular actions that the customer is taking, from an interactive standpoint. Clicking buttons, scrolling screens, tapping keys; all of these are UI elements. That should not undercut their importance in any way, and without an excellent UI, you will likely not have an excellent UX. This is where design really does tend to shine, and where functionality and ease of use of particular items becomes very important to the user.

I will emphasize again that this is not just on your website. It's anything a user interacts with to take an action as part of the product lifecycle. Opening a door is UX; the doorknob is UI. A doorknob with a nice, smooth, snappy action and good grip is good UI, for a good door-opening experience. A doorknob made out of cheese pizza is bad UI, and a bad door opening UX. Good UI isn't universal, though. In Jurassic Park, all the doors had handles. Good UI when a human uses it, bad UI when a Raptor uses it (in which the good UX is NOT being eaten). This means **Design For Your Users**!

Good UX feels effortless. Bad UX feels like work.

HANDLES: GREAT FOR HUMANS, BAD FOR RAPTORS
HUMAN PROOF
BAD UX
NOT HUMAN PROOF
GOOD UX
RAPTOR PROOF
GOOD UX
NOT RAPTOR PROOF
BAD UX

So, if it's dinner time, the UX is deciding you are hungry, driving to McDonald's, ordering through the drive thru, waiting, giving your money to the employee at window one, getting your food from the employee at window two, driving home, eating, and ultimately being full. The UI is the menu board where you order your food, or the credit card reader, or the wrapper on the burger, and how easy or difficult each one was to use becomes part of the overall experience of dinner. A good UI makes it easy to get your McNuggets. A bad UI means you can't figure out how to hold the onions on your cheeseburger. A good UX makes the entire experience from driveway to drive-thru a good one, including how long you waited in line, how nice the cashier was, and getting everything you ordered in the bag.

There's much more to UX. We have only scratched the surface when it comes to the concept. It's a good start, and enough to begin to weave the UX thread into the insurance quilt.

UX and Insurance: Why We Are Here

Just because insurance is necessary doesn't mean it escapes the need for good UX, and now it's clear that UX is about way more than just website navigation. It's every single interaction and touchpoint that your customer has with your company, across every channel, at every point in their journey: quote, in-force, cancellation, (hopefully) renewal, and back again. It's about how easy it is to pay a bill at 11 PM when the call center is closed and a live human is not available. It's how fast a claim gets processed and where the claim is along its journey. It's whether the portal works on their phone regardless of manufacturer or age of device. It's whether they trust that you know who they are when they call. It even encompasses how easy it is to find the address to (gasp) mail in a check.

This guide is about helping insurers build digital experiences that don't just meet expectations - they quietly exceed them. This guide is **not** going to be full of UX theory, detailed design guidelines, or anything that requires you to have a degree in marketing, digital media, or statistics. I'm making it approachable because that is the book that I would want to read, and because you shouldn't have to know what the Knockwust-Macaroni Effect is (yes, I made that up). If you want to learn more about UX in general, I would recommend Don Norman's *The Design of Everyday Things,* the gold standard of books on the subject, and one that sits proudly on my shelf.

Today's customers really don't need insurance to feel magical. They just need it to work like everything else in their life already does. Retail technology giants like Amazon, Netflix, and DoorDash have made it incredibly easy to get everything you have ever wanted, as soon as you want it. You no longer have to wait days for your package to arrive, spend an hour at the video rental store, or sit on a sticky plastic bench waiting for a table at your local Chili's. You can have it now! Without leaving your house! It's not just Gen Z and the TikTok generation, either. Elder millennials, Gen-X, and even some (dare I say it) boomers who grew up without instant-gratification technology have now come to expect a certain level of service from every company they interact with - including their insurer.

The Insurance UX Frontier

Of course, insurance hasn't always been the quickest to adopt and embrace new technology. It wasn't that long ago that an agent might need to **fax** an ACORD application to a carrier, just to write an auto insurance policy, and the thought of being able to find rates online from anyone beyond the top carriers was nothing more than a pipe dream. No one really expected their insurance carrier to have a good user experience. Then, all of a sudden, the future happened, and an insurer can no longer rely on the same processes, procedures, and assumptions that were relevant even five years ago. The new paradigm is that managing insurance should be as effortless as ordering a pizza, available 24/7, and entirely digital. Paper documents, mail, standard 9-5 customer service, and brick-and-mortar agents simply aren't cutting it anymore. Gartner has found that most incumbent insurers have insufficient UX strategies in place, and this means that these insurers risk losing market share to their technology-enabled competitors.

For an insurer that feels like this level of change is out of reach, and is overwhelmed by the concept of a ground-up digital transformation, it's important to truly get back to basics. Sometimes we can get so caught up in the idea of improvement for the sake of improvement that we forget to ask, what does the modern insurance customer *actually* want? Aside from their policy for free, of course. This requires a detailed and data-driven look at insurance from the perspective of the customer, and not just the perspective of the actuary, underwriter, or executive. In order to discover the true impact of the digital experience on customer behavior, we at insured.io conducted a comprehensive two-year research study that included:

A multi-question survey and analysis of 500 auto & home insurance policyholders across a variety of socio-economic and geographic backgrounds, in order to measure the influence of user experience on new customer acquisition.

A behavioral analysis of 250,000 P&C insurance customers using the insured.io omnichannel engagement

platform, to measure the influence of omnichannel, multi-channel, and single-channel digital engagement on customer retention.

The results of this study show changing perspectives, interesting trends, and bring insurance much more in-line with digital retail when assessing behavior. From policy purchasing (whether online or with an agent), to recurring billing, to claims, each step of the insurance customer journey presents its own unique challenges, expectations, experiences, and, for insurers, opportunities. Some of these notes will sound familiar, because you have likely experienced many of these strategies in other verticals that you interact with on a regular basis. For many insurers, this is still a digital frontier, and an opportunity to improve your interactions with your customers before your competitors do. Every customer that you retain is another customer that your competitors do not have. The research that we have done, as well as some time-tested strategies, show how enhanced UX / UI, digital channels, and proactive, personalized communication drive customer satisfaction, boost customer loyalty, increase revenue, decrease cost, and increase customer retention.

Part II

The Customer Journey

The Modern Insurance Odyssey

The insurance policy lifecycle encompasses every stage of a policyholder's journey - from initial quote and purchase to policy management, billing, claims, and renewal (or cancellation, but hopefully not).

For an insurer, every insured is their own Odysseus, facing multiple perils on their journey to renewal. To plan a successful journey for your insureds, you need to first build a map. Think of it as a treasure map to a satisfied customer, where X marks the spot where they renew, and each successfully completed step brings the insured that much closer to that point. A heavy-handed metaphor, yes? A good excuse for a treasure map graphic? Also yes.

THE CUSTOMER JOURNEY

Throughout this journey, an insurer has a very limited number of opportunities to make a good impression. People don't actively seek out their insurance company to interact with. Insurance is not Instagram, and people are not logging in every day to update their policy status. This means that you can't afford to have any step go wrong. Any single point of friction can damage the overall customer experience. When you plan your successful customer journey, you don't have to draw a literal map, but you should examine each step in the process, and clearly identify where your friction points might be.

First Impressions: Why Your UX Matters

Buying an insurance policy is the same as modern dating. You go on your phone, you browse through options, you find what you hope is a match, and you take your shot. And, just like dating, first impressions are everything. You put your best face forward and let your best qualities shine. You certainly don't show up to a first date wearing the outfit your mom bought you for your high school prom. When you don't keep up with the times, it shows, and you need to make sure you stay current. Here's the exciting part: you don't have to rebuild your entire infrastructure to do it.

Acquiring a new customer is expensive. According to Forbes, it's anywhere from five to seven times more costly than retaining an existing one. Given that reality, insurers can't afford to lose customers due to a frustrating or outdated digital experience.

Years ago, buying insurance meant walking into a brick-and-mortar agency or calling an agent to compare rates. But today, consumers:

Research policies online before speaking to anyone.

Compare prices AND digital experiences before making a decision.

Expect a fully online application process that doesn't require multiple steps or unnecessary friction.

With our research revealing that online experience and brand reputation are now nearly equally important when selecting an insurer, it means you can no longer just rest on having the best price, or a recognizable brand name.

When a customer drops into your website, even the average, non-technical user can tell right away, if your web presence looks like a period piece. To the average consumer that means you're old, you're slow, and you're more than likely complicated. If you are not thoughtful in your web presence, you are not going to provide a thoughtful experience throughout the rest of the journey, either. A massive 83% of people do not rate their insurance company's web presence as "excellent" - and nearly that same percentage of people actively want to manage their policy online. You have a first date with a customer every single day... is it time for you to hit the mall?

The Quote Process

A wise gecko once told us that "fifteen minutes can save you 15% or more on your car insurance." Now, I'm sure Don Draper could tell us the fundamental human reason that this ad is burned into our cultural subconscious, but that's for a book about marketing. The key here is that the message was basically "save money fast." Insurance is not exactly known for its speed, and the promise of the premise was that getting a quote was fast. The same wise gecko also told us that it was "so easy a caveman could do it." So now, we have the building blocks. Fast, easy, save money.

We are going to leave money out of the equation here, because, while good UX can actually lower your rates (better experience, higher retention, more earned premium, reduced frequency and severity… you get it), this is about your quoting process. The wise gecko's ad premiered in 1999…

which, as of this writing, must have been over one million years ago... and yet is still absolutely relevant today. Are your customers, either agents or potential insureds, able to get a quote in under 15 minutes? Under 10? Under five? If most of your business is written by agents, they will simply stop writing with your company if you're too slow. If you sell direct-to-consumer, users will get frustrated, abandon the quote, and probably never come back.

Fast and easy is not the name of the next Fast & Furious sequel (probably), but it should be your mantra when you are designing your quote flow. Of course, you need to get all necessary underwriting information, but there are smart and efficient ways to do this. Here's the part that's annoying... there is no one-size-fits-all solution. Your agents, customers, and products are all going to be a little bit different, so I can't tell you the magic solution to make your quotes fast and easy, but I can offer you some big ol' dont's.

Don't let developers design your quote flows if they don't understand your product.

Don't let underwriters design your quote flows if they only understand your product.

Don't let executives design your quote flows (with apologies to the execs reading this, but you know I'm right).

Don't let a conference room of people design your quote flows. This is chaos incarnate.

Don't listen to your customers. JUST KIDDING! This is your top priority.

The Omnichannel Experience: Cultivating Retention

So you got them in the door, what now? Once a policy is in place, customers expect to be able to easily access their policy, view details, make payments, and retrieve documents, all without having to talk to a human. Oh, and it also needs to be from anywhere, with any device. Demanding, I know. Welcome to the most crucial point in the customer journey when it comes to cultivating, growing, and harvesting retention. Once you have that customer, you want to do everything in your power to make sure that insured doesn't cancel or non-renew.

> *"We had a customer, a large, regional carrier, who had been in business since the 1800's. When we came on board, they had al-*

most no online presence whatsoever - in fact, the ONLY way to make a payment was a check, or over the phone! Deploying some simple self-service options, like automated after-hours phone payments, changed the game for them. Customer service handle times were cut in half and after hours payments skyrocketed." – an insured.io story

This is the apex point of an omnichannel strategy, where all your processes should be truly in sync, and all policy access points are given equal care and attention.

Why Omnichannel != Multichannel

When you think of omnichannel, you may think just *supporting* multiple channels for an insured - web, phone, SMS - but true omnichannel experiences create a seamless and unified experience, via these channels, throughout the entire process.

A simple example of bad omnichannel: an auto insurer has developed multiple portals, over time, from multiple different vendors. They have finally modernized their online quote flow, and it is slick. The insured buys a policy, and is impressed by the ease with which their policy was bound. Then they register for an online account in order to pay their first bill. This platform was built five years ago, and shares no connective tissue with the awesome quote flow. It's difficult to register, is barely mobile friendly, and clearly looks its age. As an insurer, you may think, well, we have an online quote flow, we have an online portal, we are supporting the important channels, right? In this case, the post-bind experience for the insured, who has to log-in multiple times per year, has been soured, and that customer is much less likely to stay with you long-term.

This is not a fabricated experience. When digital transformation becomes a large ordeal, and is done over multiple years, you can end up with a mix of technologies. Omnichannel, yes, but true omnichannel? Not at all.

This is the first step in truly understanding that just because, as an insurer, you DO a thing, does not mean that that thing is the right thing. A seamless, unified, digital-first approach ensures that customers can easily engage with their policy, enhancing satisfaction, retention, and overall experience; made better when the experience is truly omnichannel, that being, channels are accessible, synchronized, and, to borrow from Gen-Z, should really all have the same vibe.

Listening to Data: How User Feedback Transforms Experience

Customer behavior can often be unpredictable, which highlights the importance of making data-driven decisions in product development. Assumptions about how users will interact with a product can be misleading. For instance, when we launched our Insured Portal in 2019, we believed we had a solid understanding of our users' needs and preferences. Despite this, we encountered unexpected challenges based on our own biases about interface design.

We were confident that the placement of insurance ID cards under the "Documents" tab was intuitive. However, customer feedback soon revealed that many users found it difficult to locate their ID cards, which was surprising to us. This feedback prompted us to analyze usage data, an essential practice for understanding user interaction. Our analysis showed that placing a primary function like retrieving an ID card behind a seemingly unrelated section was hindering the user experience.

To address this, we added a direct link in the main menu labeled "ID Cards," which led to the same location as the "Documents" link. This small, yet significant change made the function more transparent and accessible. The result was a dramatic increase in user adoption and a cessation of complaints about this issue. This experience reinforced the value of a data-driven approach to design, showing how vital it is to align product features with actual user behavior.

This scenario underscores a common oversight in the executive decision-making process, where choices about user behavior and "best practices" are often made at a high level, detached from the actual user experience and based on outdated or incorrect assumptions. To truly serve users effectively, it's crucial to dive deep into the specifics of their interactions—what they are doing, when they are doing it, how long they engage, and most importantly, why they behave in certain ways. Understanding these elements can guide more informed, user-centered design decisions and lead to better product outcomes. This approach not only enhances user satisfaction but also drives more efficient and effective use of resources in developing and refining digital tools.

The importance of customer engagement is increasingly recognized across industries. According to the "State of Customer Engagement Report" from Twilio, 76% of businesses stated that customer engagement is a critical priority in 2024. This statistic underscores the shifting focus towards customer-centric strategies in business planning. Emphasizing customer engagement not only fosters greater customer loyalty but also propels companies towards more dynamic and responsive product development. Integrating customer feedback and data analytics is not just a tactical move—it's a strategic imperative that can significantly influence the success of digital platforms and services.

Payments: The #1 Way You Get Money

You can't keep your policyholders if you can't take their money! Making a payment is the top reason insurance customers log into their portal, and for auto and homeowner's policyholders, they may need to make that payment each and every month. This means customers will demand an easy, fast, secure way to make digital payments - and mistakes when it comes to payments can cost an insurer.

Paying bills can be painful for many consumers, so any experience should make the bill-paying process as simple as possible. A self-service digital payment option allows customers to pay their bills when convenient for them, whether during normal business hours or in the middle of the night on a holiday, and the payment experience should be the same whether they talk to a human, call on the phone, send a text, or log-in online. Payments themselves are a micro-journey, and the UX of invoice to payment is equally as important as quote to renewal... in fact, one begets the other. You should never make it difficult for someone to pay you. This starts from the invoice itself. The mail you send the insured is still part of the overall experience. Take a look at your invoices and ask yourself, "If I got this in the mail, would I understand it?". In particular, remember that most people don't know insurance, the word "premium" means "best", and all fees are bad. I

Clearly define what is owed on invoices. If they don't understand the bill, they will call you.

Make starting a payment easy. Don't use some obscure data element to validate them.

Send automated SMS & email reminders. People forget!

Allow multiple payment methods, in addition to e-check and credit card, like Apple Pay.

Absolutely make it easy to sign up for Autopay. You want your money on time every month?

Basically, never slouch on your payment processes! You need

money to buy cubicles, office chairs, printer paper, coffee, and to pay your employees, and claims... not necessarily in that order.

Text-To-Pay: Gimmick or Genius?

With so many payment options, you may think that paying with a text message might be at the bottom of the list. In fact, Text-To-Pay has grown exponentially in recent years, and this is because it has a real advantage - it's super easy! It's also where a truly connected experience shines. An insured receives a text message, letting them know they have a bill due. They reply to that message, which walks them through a payment process. That credit card that they saved in their wallet on the portal? They can easily use that to complete the payment with a text. It's quick, secure, doesn't require remembering complex passwords, and can be done from anywhere there is a cell signal. Everyone texts, and utilizing the channels that your customers ACTUALLY use... well that's just good business.

Retention & Loyalty with Outbound Engagement

Retention isn't achieved by crossing your fingers and hoping the policy renews or doesn't cancel. It's consistent, proactive engagement that keeps your brand top of mind, builds trust, and makes sticking with you a no-brainer.

A dialed-in outbound engagement strategy means reaching out before customers think to reach out to you. Whether it's billing reminders, renewal notices, proactive claims updates, or personalized policy recommendations, every touchpoint strengthens retention. Communication goes beyond just policy information as well. You can personalize content "just for them," with helpful tips, ways to save money, and even weather notifications.

So, what are the best ways to stay ahead of churn and keep policyholders engaged?

A strong retention strategy doesn't wait until renewal time to check in. It builds consistent, value-driven communication throughout the entire policy lifecycle. There's a saying where I come from: "Doing something is always better than doing nothing" (editors note: this is not a saying where he comes from). So, do something!

> *"In the early 2010's, nobody was doing automated outreach for retention. When we piloted it, in non-standard auto, we saw the numbers drastically change. Cancellation decreases 5-10% and reinstatements, almost the same. As it turns out, there's a science to being annoying, and just annoying enough to remind them to pay their bill." – an insure d.io story*

The Most Impactful Retention Messaging Includes:

Welcome Messages – A simple "Thanks for choosing us!"

goes a long way in setting expectations and ensuring customers know how to access their policy details, payments, and self-service options.

Billing Reminders & Payment Notices – Timing matters. Proactive SMS and email reminders ensure customers don't lapse simply because they forgot a due date.

Renewal Outreach – Customers need multiple touchpoints leading up to renewal. A single notice isn't enough - especially when people are flooded with renewal offers from competitors.

Claims Follow-Ups – A well-timed post-claims follow-up message helps measure customer satisfaction, address concerns, and build long-term loyalty.

Part III

The Claims Experience

Get Your 3D Glasses on

As we all know, every good part 3 should be in 3D. Jaws 3D, Friday the 13 Part 3-D, the rest. Of course this part 3 is no different. With claims, there are only 3 D's that you need to know: **Define, Domino's, and Dollars**. I know it's a bit of a stretch for a joke, but in reality, the next few sections address important key points in the claims process, and ones that you need to pay attention to. So pop on those 3D Glasses (sold separately) and let the claims experience come straight at you. Just don't drop the popcorn.

Claims Define Your Brand

Your claims experience is hands-down one of the most important ways to define your brand. How insureds experience the claims process shapes their public reviews and brand perception, and a bad claims experience can erase years of customer loyalty in an instant. Unfortunately, the claims process tends to be a big black box of mystery, and insureds often have no way to peek behind the proverbial curtain.

> *"We had a customer who had a 1 star Google ranking - I'm not sure it can even go lower than that. Their claims experience wasn't even that bad, but the vocal minority drove their rankings down, with nearly every negative review about their claims process. It took a massive outbound campaign to drive that*

ranking up, just to balance out the poor reviews!" – an insured.io story

First Notice of Loss & Claims Intake

When a customer has a claim they need to file, regardless of the line of business, they are probably in a pretty bad mood. Crashed cars and trees through windows can be frustrating things to deal with, and they always seem to happen at the worst times. When these situations happen, the absolute last thing anyone wants to do is deal with their insurance company.

As an insurer, claims are a complex subject. On one hand, the fewer claims that are paid out, the better. From a purely bottom line perspective, it doesn't exactly make sense to make the process incredibly smooth. And yet, from the human perspective, we understand that these moments are exactly why insurance exists, and why we all have jobs, and even why you are reading this today. Your company lives and breathes on its ability to gain new customers and keep existing ones, while, of course, maintaining excellent loss ratios. This means a smooth claims experience, and a smooth claims experience starts with claims intake.

Claims reporting can vary so wildly from company to company and from LOB to LOB that there is barely any way to make a generalization, but companies like Progressive can have you draw the path of an accident directly on a map on your screen, while another company might have a form, and another still a PDF, and someone else a M-F 9-5 phone number. If you are reading this, and you are thinking. "Hey Steve, my form is great," then it actually might be a clunky and outdated process. A low-tech process delays response times and leaves insureds frustrated. Without a digitally enabled claims intake, response times can stretch for days, causing confusion and stress. This is bad UX! Now the bad Yelp reviews, now the decrease in retention... you get the point.

Streamlined digital claims intake is a must. You don't have to be Progressive, but you do have to be progressive. Insureds should be able to submit a claim online, with data immediately delivered to your claims system for processing. After-hours claims should automatically route to digital intake for faster resolution. Filing a claim should be fast, easy, and painless. Remember, this insured is not happy to be doing this, so do them a solid, since they may pay you thousands of dollars per year, and take it easy on them. It needs to be intuitive and easy to navigate. It needs to make sense. It needs to not require a bunch of info that no person is actually going to have. And one of the absolute most important... if you are asking insureds for industry jargon like "Please list perils," or "is this a comprehensive or a collision claim," then you are a jerk.

The faster and simpler the submission process, the sooner a claims rep can make contact. The sooner a claim can get started, the sooner it can be finished, and the insured can move on. During the claims process, however, there are additional struggles.

Claims Updates

"What's going on with my claim?"

This is a question that customer service representatives hear far too often. It's estimated that 30-40% of customer service calls are regarding a claim's status. As we have discussed, when a person is in the midst of a claim, they could be without a vehicle, in a damaged house, even injured... and they just want to know when they can be made whole again. It's human nature to question everything, doubly so when it comes to money.

Nearly 60% of policyholders would switch insurers just for timely updates on their claims. That loyalty you have worked so hard to earn through every other method can be gone in an instant when you start impacting their financial well-being. Simply put, insureds need updates. In a perfect world, a human would be able to call everyone who has a claim and walk them through the process, and be able to return calls and emails within the hour. In reality, claims departments are just as busy as the general customer service department, and this is where a digital helping hand is necessary.

An effective strategy for digital claims updates is twofold. The first is *proactive notifications*. This means that when a new milestone is reached, such as, "Your adjuster has been assigned," or "Your estimate is in progress," a notification should go out via email and/or SMS. This gives insureds the answers they need before they need to call and ask. The second is *claims tracking*, which gives the insured the ability to find exactly what step in the claims process they are currently on, what that step means, and what the next step likely is. Usually visually, and usually from within the insured portal. In the following section, we give an illustration of how this was solved - by a restaurant of all places - using something called "operational transparency."

These types of updates aren't just a convenience; they are a meaningful tool to reduce call center volume, increase customer satisfaction, and improve retention.

There's no hard and fast rule here when it comes to technology. The experience can and will vary from line of business to line of business, but no matter what, it needs to be seamless. A seamless claims experience doesn't just improve satisfaction - it builds trust and long-term loyalty.

Your Claim is in the Oven: What Insurers Should Learn from Domino's Pizza Tracker

In 2009, Domino's Pizza was in trouble. The pizza was bad, their image was worse, and their sales and market share were abysmal. Domino's was practically a swear word when it came time to suggest a pizza place.

Transparency and Innovation Save a Brand

In 2010, with a new CEO on board and practically nothing to lose, Domino's opted for a unique and somewhat terrifying solution: complete transparency. The company admitted that their pizza's quality was poor and promised to improve. They apologized to the masses, and the masses responded in kind. People loved their transparent approach, the brutal honesty, and the promise to be better.

Since then, they have seen nearly a 3x growth in revenue and have reached nearly 20% of total pizza sales. With this focus on transparency, Domino's also launched what some consider to be one of the most significant UX features of all time - the Pizza Tracker. Yes, the colorful little widget that tracks your pizza's journey from dough to doorstep. This innovation, which today seems so ubiquitous, was revolutionary at launch; a unique marriage of logistics to food service, combined with the dopamine hit of knowing that "Tim has placed your pizza in the oven."

Nearly every industry has implemented some version of the Pizza Tracker, to various degrees of success. Uber and Amazon show your driver's precise location on a digital map of your city, while USPS lets you know that, for some reason, your package is in Bakersfield, CA instead of your house.

Your Claim is Ready: Lessons from Domino's

In classic "late to the party" fashion, insurance lacks its own version of the Pizza Tracker. As silly as it may sound, insurers can learn much from Domino's.

In a previous section, we learned that nearly 60% of policyholders would switch insurers just for timely updates on their claims. This clearly shows that there is a need for **operational transparency** during the claims process. Operational transparency, like an open restaurant kitchen, can be implemented in various ways across every industry.

Price transparency can lead to over a 26% increase in sales, and revealing your processes behind the scenes can increase perception of quality and willingness to pay. A pizza delivery from Domino's is cheap when compared to a damaged vehicle or home; however, you are infinitely more likely to know exactly where your pizza is than where your claim payment is.

The numbers show us that insureds hate being left in the dark during a claim. This uncertainty leads to frustration, which leads to a flood of inbound calls, chats, and emails, asking, "What's going on with my claim?"

Eventually, this frustration can lead to losing the insured altogether.

The Return Trip Effect

The Pizza Tracker reduces frustration by immediately adding operational transparency. When a person feels like they are a part of the process, rather than simply a bystander, it ultimately creates a sense that the entire system is moving faster. Shuya Gong, a design director at IDEO, believes that the Pizza Tracker has an effect of "speeding up time" because of the return trip effect, the feeling that time moves faster on the way back from a destination. Once you understand the duration of a journey, the perceived time it takes to complete goes down. This is why progress bars on downloads and file transfers have existed since the dawn of computer graphics. They are a visual time machine for the user.

The insurance industry is primed for a similar experience of transparency. There are a finite number of steps to a claim, from first notice of loss to final payout. Displaying all those steps locks in the duration of the claims journey, at least in terms of the number of steps. This creates the progress bar that both pizza lovers and insureds crave.

Data and Display

Implementing a Pizza Tracker ideology within your insured portal is a two-part process: Data and Display. Data comes from your claims or policy systems, where the status of a claim must be captured, so it can be utilized. Constructing an API or a data extraction process to gain access to this data is vitally important. Once the data is exposed, it needs to be displayed to the insured in a way that makes sense and follows the Pizza Tracker model. It doesn't need to **look** exactly like Domino's, but it should show a complete timeline of all of the steps of a claim.

Most importantly, it needs to show what step they are currently on, and any relevant information associated with that step. If the adjuster has been assigned, display their contact information. If it's at the Body Shop, give the name and phone number. If you don't have all the data, that's OK.

Even if there is a 10% reduction in claims calls, that can become a real-world savings of thousands of dollars. Luckily, there are many third-party tools and platforms that can help make this process much easier to implement, so you don't have to reinvent the wheel.

Leveraging Multiple Channels

A Pizza Tracker-type of experience for insurers doesn't always have to be visual. Once you have access to an insured's data, you can offer something as simple as proactive notifications, primarily with SMS, and backed up by email.

Sending messages like, "Your adjuster has been assigned," or "Your estimate is in progress," keeps policyholders in the loop and informed without requiring them to click anything.

DoorDash has a similar concept; they use every means of communication they have to update the status of a food delivery. They do this, along with sharing a map, to reduce customer frustration over delivery times and prevent complaints. That's why these types of updates aren't just an added convenience; they reduce call center volume, take the pressure off of claims reps, increase customer satisfaction, and ultimately improve retention.

None of this is a revolutionary idea today. However, insurers can leverage innovations from the consumer world to gain a better understanding of the human need for visualizing progress and build a better claims experience. Keep in mind that not all of the insurance lifecycle needs to be exposed to the public, as there is little desire to "see into the kitchen" of many other insurance processes.

During the claims process, if insurers can keep policyholders updated, informed, and show them where their money is, they will have a happier customer. No one expects their claim to be paid in "30 minutes or it's free," the pizza guys can keep that one, but when it comes to the customer journey, insurers can learn a lot from Domino's.

Claims & Outbound Payments

The final step in the claims journey, and the part of the claims process that usually feels like watching paint dry: the actual payment. The claim is complete, all parties are satisfied, and now it's time to get you your check. Yes, I said check. As in "Pay to the order of" on a piece of paper. Historically, insurers have mailed this physical check to you, sometimes days (or weeks) after the claim has been approved. That's... fine, I guess. If it's 1998. But in a world where someone can Venmo their roommate for tacos in four seconds, sending a paper check in the mail feels like a joke - one the customer isn't laughing at.

Even with next-day air from FedEx, there is still a lot that can happen between send and receive, so why leave it up to chance? Even once the check is received and deposited, the receiving bank may take days to clear the money. In that amount of time, the insured's rental car coverage is done, and the raccoons that lived in the tree have moved into the guest room.

It's interesting how many insurers have technologically advanced the process of collecting premium, but the reverse had, for many years, stagnated. The final step in the claims journey should not be the one where the ball is dropped. Today's digital claims payment options are faster, smarter, and actually aligned with how people live. Funds can be deposited directly to a bank account, loaded onto a prepaid debit card, pushed to a digital wallet, or even crypto. Insureds can even choose their preferred method. That flexibility not only improves satisfaction - it removes unnecessary friction from a process that's already emotional and time-sensitive.

Speed matters. When a customer is dealing with the stress of an auto accident or a property loss, getting paid quickly can completely change how they perceive the experience. A digital-first payment strategy doesn't just close the loop faster - it builds trust, reduces call volume, and gives the customer one less thing to worry about.

So yes, you still *can* mail a check. But should you? Let's just say... if your competitors aren't doing it, your customers won’t wait around while you do.

Part IV

Building Great UX

Four Principles of Great UX

User experience in insurance isn't about pixel-perfect design or Silicon Valley buzzwords. It's about making things simple, fast, and human - for people who are often dealing with something stressful, boring, or both.

Great UX doesn't mean customers *notice* how slick your portal is. It means they don't have to think about it at all. The best experiences feel invisible: no friction, no confusion, no frustration. Just done.

Across everything we've built, tested, and studied, great insurance UX boils down to four key principles:

1. Consistency Across Channels

Your quoting flow, portal, billing system, and claims center should feel like one connected experience, not a scavenger hunt across five vendors.

2. Speed + Simplicity

Every extra click, field, or login is an opportunity for the customer to bail. Shorten the path. Eliminate noise. Prioritize action over process.

3. Personalization with Purpose

Show customers that you know who they are. Use data to offer relevant choices, default to smart settings, and tailor communications to their situation - not just their policy type.

4. Mobile-First, Self-Serve Always

Your customers expect to do everything from their phone. That includes paying bills, checking coverage, submitting claims, and asking questions. If they can't do it from the couch, they won't do it at all.

These principles guide the pages ahead - whether we're talking about portals, IVR, or payment UX. You don't need to reinvent your business. You just need to start designing it around the people who actually use it.

So, where do most customers *actually* experience your UX? Let's start with the thing they need to use the most: the Insured Portal.

Insured Portal: Digital Front Door

Your public facing website is your front yard - it has to have good curb appeal, it has to be informative, but ultimately, it's only a single part of your entire online experience. Your insured portal and/or your mobile app is your true front door. Once we open that door, you better be ready for what's coming. It will be the main place that your customers go when they need help, need answers, need to make a payment before midnight, and need their documents. That means it has to **work**, and it has to make sense. We have talked much in the way of UX theory, but we haven't talked much about true features.

Prioritizing the Right Features in Your Portal

With endless customization options, insurers must focus on what truly matters in a digital portal. 87% of policyholders access their insurance via mobile devices, so a mobile-first design isn't optional - it's essential. Keeping customer data secure is non-negotiable, but other must-have features include:

Seamless mobile compatibility for 24/7 access.

Integrated payments that are quick and hassle-free.

Simple claim submission & real-time tracking.

Proactive alerts for billing, renewals, and severe weather.

Data-driven recommendations tailored to policyholder needs.

Understanding Customer Needs

A portal should be built around how customers actually use it. The top reasons policyholders engage with their insurer? Billing, policy support, and claim status. Prioritizing these areas ensures immediate value and reduces unnecessary customer frustration. A common fallacy among insurers is that a low premium is enough for their customers. After all, insurance is a commoditized industry, and in many cases, it's legally required; and a captive audience can be pushed around quite a bit, right? I'm here to tell you that the commoditization of insurance is quickly going away, and it's time to start understanding customer needs.

User Experience & Personalization

Consumers expect simple, intuitive, and frictionless experiences - just like the apps they use daily. A well-designed portal should be easy to navigate and reflect the insurer's brand.

Personalization is a must. A McKinsey study found that 71% of consumers expect tailored interactions, yet 76% get frustrated when they don't receive them. Insurers who leverage customer data to provide relevant content, customized recommendations, and proactive messaging will create an experience that keeps customers engaged - and loyal. For example, you can tell them that there is a recall on their vehicle, that a storm is headed their way, and remind them to change their air filter. Use your data as a tool to build personalized experiences.

What Makes an Insured Portal "Excellent"?

Realistically, the barrier to an excellent customer experience really isn't that high.

Mobile-friendly, intuitive interface - as seamless as other modern apps.

Integrated payments - no extra logins required.

Personalized recommendations - tailored content based on the customer's needs.

Ultimately, a well-designed insured portal directly reduces call center volume, increases retention, and improves the overall customer experience.

IVR: When Phones Still Matter

Interactive Voice Response (IVR) has long been a core part of insurance customer service, but traditional IVR systems often frustrate more than they assist. Outdated menus, rigid phone trees, and long wait times, as well as voice prompts that absolutely can not understand you, have conditioned many customers to avoid IVR whenever possible.

Yet, voice communication is everywhere. With Alexa, Siri and Google today's consumers are more comfortable engaging via voice than ever before. Insurers who modernize their IVR systems can turn this channel into a powerful, automated, and highly personalized customer experience tool. This is a place where AI can truly shine, using it as a tool to generate human sounding voices and natural feeling workflows.

Prioritizing the Right Features in Your IVR

A well-built IVR should do more than just route calls - it should actively resolve customer issues, streamline self-service, and create a better experience for both policyholders and customer service representatives. Consider actions that are simple for a CSR to do, and apply those to the IVR, such as receiving an ID card, inquiring about policy status, or enrolling in SMS notifications.

User Experience & Personalization

Just like a digital portal, an IVR experience should feel effortless, intuitive, and personalized. Customers expect technology to anticipate their needs, not force them through endless menu options. Additionally, we talked about personalization in the previous section, and those statements hold true with the IVR as well.

The Biggest Customer Frustrations

Speech Recognition – Despite what every automated system you ever call would have you believe, no one wants to yell "REPRESENTATIVE" at their phone. More importantly, poor speech recognition is not accessible to those that speak a different language or have an accent, which can disenfranchise many insureds.

Nonsense Workflows – A labyrinth of keypresses that ultimately leads you nowhere, or back to the beginning, and is not optimized for basic interactions, is the death knell for any IVR system.

Difficult to understand - IVRs using a poor voice engine are impossible to understand, slow, and frustrating to your average consumer.

Lacking self-service capabilities – If the IVR can't handle basic requests like checking a balance or policy renewal date, it might as well just be a hold queue.

The Must-Have Features of a Modern IVR:

Personalization – Recognizes callers and pulls up relevant policy details in real-time, reducing the need for customers to verify information repeatedly.

Multi-language and accessibility support – A smart IVR can seamlessly handle multiple languages, accents, and provide better support for the hearing and visually impaired.

Self-service options – IVR should allow customers to

make a payment, check claim status, update policy details, or request documents - all without speaking to an agent.

A well-optimized IVR reduces the burden on call center agents, allowing them to focus on higher-value customer interactions.

What Makes an IVR System "Excellent"?

To transform IVR from a necessary evil into a customer service asset, insurers must ensure their system is:

Smart and Context-Aware – Recognizes returning callers, understands their needs, and provides relevant, automated responses.

Flexible and Efficient – Offers accessibility, multilingual support, and effortless navigation.

Seamlessly Integrated with Other Channels – Syncs with portals, SMS, and customer service to provide a cohesive omnichannel experience.

Designed to Reduce Call Center Strain – Resolves routine inquiries instantly while ensuring complex cases are escalated to human agents efficiently.

A modern IVR system doesn't just handle calls - it enhances the entire customer experience, reduces operational costs, and strengthens policyholder relationships. A poorly designed IVR doesn't just frustrate customers - it actively damages your brand perception. If you don't believe me, go hop on the /r/customerservice subreddit and see how many people colorfully describe their frustrations. Actually, maybe don't do that - we don't encourage doomscrolling here.

Virtual Agents, Chatbots, and AI

Nothing is going to date this entire book more than a chapter on AI. I'm writing this in 2025, so if any single section is going to justify me putting out the occasional "Revised Edition"... it's this section right here. AI is changing everything that we do at an astronomical pace: the way we do business, the way we write code, the way we compose emails, and it's at a state where its ability to truly warp reality (deepfakes, virtual humans, video) is still being explored. So, where does all this fit in with insurance? I considered not adding this section at all, because I think any discussion about how to "properly" use AI in insurance is bound to be a hot take, but there *are* some fundamental ways I believe that it can enhance your UX strategy. Keyword, "enhance"... not replace.

Implementing AI right at the front line of your customer

service is an extremely useful tool, when used properly. This is what I like to call Responsible AI. As an insurer, you want to make sure that you control the flow of any customer journey. The "happy path" is the workflow or workflows that get the customer exactly where they need to go, and accomplish exactly what they want to accomplish, in the most efficient way possible. This means a combined strategy of well-designed workflows mixed with AI that interprets a customer's intention, in order to consistently and quickly funnel the user to the correct spot.

The AI funnel is important because humans are entirely unpredictable. Let's say that you ask them for their policy number in order to look up their information. A traditional workflow requires that they specifically enter "POL123456-1", or something to that effect, so that lookup can work. With the power of AI as an interpretive tool, they can enter "hello, my policy number is POL123456-1, thank you" and a well-trained AI can interpret the intention, strip out the unnecessary data, and pass that in to you API or whatever exists behind the scenes. In this case, the AI doesn't control the workflow, it improves the experience with very specific training. A chatbot that is more generically trained might still get them to the same place, but it also may not... if the workflow is completely left to AI, while this can be done, you potentially risk the "happy path" being the "long and confusing path."

Since customers can easily become frustrated, AI Agents must be trained to properly hand off to a human at the slightest bit of confusion. This process is called "Human-In-The-Loop" (HITL) and is vitally important for customer satisfaction, avoiding Doom Loops and ultimately the customer giving up. And, for the sake of every one, make sure the Agent can only answer questions relevant to your business. There are too many examples of people typing strange requests into a prompt and your chatbot now becomes a strange GPT hybrid that goes off the rails. Ultimately, this means that the "AI" part of the virtual agent should be additive rather than reductive to your existing workflows.

Really, there are four reasons that a customer is reaching out to you. The customer needs to know very quickly that they can accomplish these tasks, and you need to know their goal very quickly in order to funnel them to the right place.

The first is to make a payment. If your Agent can't take payments (many don't), make that clear early in the process. The second reason is to file a claim. With this, it's important to quickly get them to the right place, whether that is an online FNOL process, a phone number, or an email address, they should be able to do that without frustration. Third, they need something. Could be a dec page, an ID card, or general information. Can you move them quickly to the insured portal? Can you auto email a document? Fourth, they need to make a policy change. That is not the job for an AI Agent, at least not yet, so here, along with possibly reason 3, is where you need to implement HITL or quickly direct them to the right place to reach their end goal.

Ultimately, this is all in the service of a better user experience. When you hand off little tasks to AI (or any other self-service tool, for that matter) you give that customer back a little bit of that time they would have spent on the phone, and you give that CSR back a little bit more time to help a customer that really needs it. AI decision-making can route claims faster, point users to the right section of a website, read and analyze complex documents, consume infinite amounts of data, and answer all kinds of questions... just don't replace your humans with it quite yet.

Part V

A New Beginning

Where to Start: High-Impact, Low-Lift Moves

You've made it this far - so, let's talk about what can actually move the needle.

Improving insurance UX doesn't require an army of developers or a total core system overhaul. Most of the biggest wins come from addressing the obvious friction points your customers are already complaining about. And if they're not complaining, they're quietly leaving. These strategies are designed to give you practical ways to spot those moments and fix them - without waiting for next year's roadmap. You don't need a moonshot project to improve customer experience.

Here are a few "low-code / no-code" upgrades that will make your policyholders feel like you're actually listening:

Modernize Your Payment Flow: Add Apple Pay, Google Pay, or saved card options. Embed it into your portal or use text-to-pay. Just stop making them log in twice.

Add Voice: People will always call your customer service line. Give them the ability to self-service over the phone without hanging up and going somewhere else.

Turn On Proactive SMS Messaging: Billing reminders, claims status, welcome messages. These are automated, inexpensive, and expected.

Unify the Visual Language: If your quote page looks slick but your portal looks like Windows 95, customers *notice*. Align branding, fonts, and flows across platforms.

Simplify Claims Intake: Ask fewer questions. Don't make them learn insurance jargon. Start with one big, "Tell us what happened" text box, then guide them forward.

The UX Survival Kit Checklist

Every insurer should ask themselves some questions when reviewing their customer journey. Below are a few general examples to get you going (although if you can't confidently say "yes" to most of these, that's your first to-do list). This section could also be called "Customer Journey KPIs" as well; we are just trying to measure success. Sure, there's NPS scores, and you should definitely get to those... but it doesn't have to be today. I left you some space to write your own in. Don't cheat and write it after you have solved it like I do with my Trello board (I love to complete a work item) but really stop and think about where you would like your customer experience to be in six months.

□ Can a customer complete a quote in under 10 minutes?

□ Can a customer make a mobile payment with one hand?

□ Are all your digital channels working together seamlessly?

□ Do your self-service options speed up the process?

□ Do you truly put your best foot forward at every point in the customer journey?

Add Your Own

- ☐ ____________________
- ☐ ____________________
- ☐ ____________________
- ☐ ____________________

The Outbound Retention Playbook

Engagement fuels engagement. If you're not proactively reaching out to customers, you're already losing them.

Welcome messages set the tone. Send a low-cost welcome message to ensure policyholders have all the info they need before their first bill arrives.

Personalization matters. Generic messages get ignored. Use names, policy details, and relevant offers to keep customers engaged.

Balance persistence with tact. Reminders should be effective, not overwhelming. Your goal is to be first on their list to get paid - not first on their block list.

Align with paycheck cycles. Timing matters. Target retention campaigns around common payroll dates when customers are more likely to pay their bills.

Send messages when people are actually available. Batching emails at midnight? Bad idea. Messages should hit inboxes during waking hours when policyholders are likely to see them.

Expect call-backs at key times. Morning messages = lunch-hour responses. Afternoon reminders = early evening calls. Plan staffing accordingly.

Stagger outbound efforts. Sending 10,000 messages at once? Expect 10,000 responses at once. Spreading them out avoids overwhelming your call center.

Pre, during, and post-cancellation messaging. Customers don't always pay on time. Strategic messaging before, during, and after cancellation periods improves retention.

Automate, Engage, Retain. The formula is simple. Automated engagement leads to automatic retention.

Part VI

The TLDR

Too Long, Didn't Read

Look, I get it. You're busy. Maybe you read the whole thing, maybe you skipped to the end to find out whodunnit (the butler, candlestick, conservatory, you know the drill). Either way, here's the survival recap - the key ideas you need to stay alive in the new insurance landscape:

Expectations Have Changed

Customers aren't comparing you to other insurers anymore. They're comparing you to Amazon, Netflix, and DoorDash. If your digital experience feels clunky, outdated, or slow, they won't stick around.

UX Is the Real Differentiator

Price and coverage still matter, sure - but user experience is what wins (and keeps) customers. A seamless, digital-first journey is no longer a luxury. It's table stakes.

Omnichannel Isn't Optional

It's not enough to offer multiple channels. They have to work together, feel connected, and share the same *vibe*. Your quoting flow and billing portals should not exist in different decades.

Claims and Payments Make or Break Loyalty

FNOL needs to be fast, intuitive, and digital. And when it's time to pay the claim? Drop the checkbook. Today's customers expect their money *now*, in the way they prefer.

Self-Service Is the Default

87% of policyholders access their account on mobile. If your insureds can't pay a bill, check their coverage, or update their policy on the go, you're risking churn.

Retention Starts With Outreach

Proactive communication - before, during, and after key events - builds trust and drives retention. Engagement fuels engagement. Silence fuels cancellations.

You Don't Have to Rebuild Everything

Start with the parts of your experience that create the most friction. Small wins in billing, claims, or communications can have a huge impact. You don't need a full transformation to deliver a better experience.

The question isn't if your digital experience needs an upgrade. The question is: Are you ready to meet customer expectations - before they switch to someone who will?

Research Insights

What matters most when picking an insurer (%)

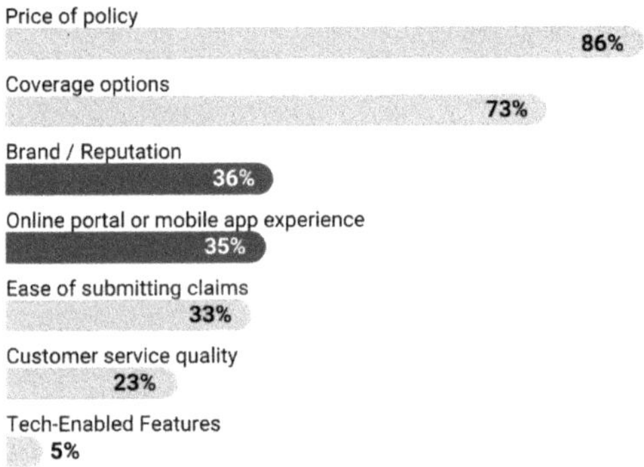

Insureds who would switch insurers to one that provided timely claims alerts

Insureds that prefer digital channels (%)

About the author

Steve Johnson is the Co-Founder and Chief Product Officer of insured.io, a company focused on improving the customer journey and accelerating digital transformation for insurance organizations. In his current role, he has led the charge in building insured.io's unique and powerful platform, maintaining overarching responsibility for the organization's product, design, development, analytics, and marketing in order to continuously innovate and deploy high-quality solutions for insurers. He is also the Founder of hibackpack.com, a travel insurance brand that aims to disrupt the way US travelers buy their travel insurance.

Before founding insured.io, Steve held software development and underwriting roles across both personal and commercial lines insurance companies. With more than two decades of industry experience and a background in full-stack software development, art, and design, he brings a unique blend of technical and creative expertise. He earned a Bachelor of Arts in History from California State University, Sacramento, and is a Pragmatic Certified Product Manager. Outside of work, Steve enjoys all forms of analog media, 1980s horror, hard science fiction, and meticulously tracking every film he's ever watched on Letterboxd.

Steve can be reached by email at steve@insured.io or on LinkedIn at https://www.linkedin.com/in/steve-johnson--

www.ingramcontent.com/pod-product-compliance
Lightning Source LLC
LaVergne TN
LVHW050938210926
848482LV00013B/654

* 9 7 9 8 2 1 8 8 4 7 0 7 4 *